A Beautiful Heart

Arun Warikoo

BlueRose Publishers

First Published in December 2020

ISBN: 978-93-5427-137-3

BLUEROSE PUBLISHERS
www.bluerosepublishers.com
info@bluerosepublishers.com
+91 8882 898 898

Cover Design:
Jasleen Ashta

Typographic Design:
Ilma Mirza

Distributed by: BlueRose, Amazon, Flipkart, Shopclues

Dedicated to

mom and dad, who wanted me to write

my wife Koko, who believed in it

my lovely daughters Aaradhya and Aadhya

and to my readers

Special thanks to Aaradhya for helping me with some of the sketches

FOREWORD

I have known Arun from his childhood. Even as a child, unlike his sibling and cousins, he was calm, composed, and contemplative. It gives me great joy to learn, from reading his first poetry collection, 'A Beautiful Heart', that he has not only retained all the qualities he possessed as a child, but also enhanced these manifold.

'A Beautiful Heart' is an unusual collection in many ways for it is concise and uncomplicated, unlike the poetry that we come to read these days. At a time when poetry is overflowing with bitterness, negativity, heartbreaks and conceit, Arun's poems evoke an old world charm which is both reassuring and propitious.

Both in structure and content, Arun retains a childlike simplicity and honesty in his poetry. These poems speak of a time when life was simple and sweet; when spirituality was an integral part of one's very being; when nature was benevolent;

when humanity was the dominant subject-matter of poetry. These poems must be read for their compassion and faith in the goodness of humankind.

Ravinder Kaul
Cultural Critic

PREFACE

My poetic journey started in 2016 when I wrote my first poem "Shiva". Over these years, I have written many more in English, Hindi and Urdu.

and then, *A Beautiful Heart* happened ...

This brings us to the question, what is real beauty?

It is a combination of a good heart and a virtuous soul. A person with high ideals, noble thoughts and positive spirit is beautiful from both within and without. *A Beautiful Heart* faces challenges with aplomb and is a source of inspiration for others to follow. His or her very presence brings happiness and a positive vibe that wins the hearts of people.

"Everything has beauty, but not everyone sees it", so says Confucius.

A person with *A Beautiful Heart* sees beauty in everything around him, be it family or connecting with nature. Such soul is truly spiritual with tremendous inner strength.

A Beautiful Heart captures the feelings of real beauty. This collection of forty five poems is written on four themes – family bonds, spirituality, nature, and inner strength. This book is a journey that explores powerful emotions and experiences that each one of us go through in our lifetime.

I hope with all my heart that you will like these poems and will be able to relate with them in one way or the other.

Happy Reading!

Much love and peace.
Arun Warikoo

CONTENTS

FAMILY BONDS

DAD

he is a man of honor
with a heart of gold
that is my dad
his story needs to be told

he prompts me to leap
goals that seem out of touch
such an inspiration
I look up to him so much

he is with me
through thick and thin
tough from outside
but is a softie within

MOM

I remember my days as a kid
those super human things you did
the warmth of your touch
the selfless love and care

the best teacher by far
an incredible counsel you are
you are my pillar of strength
forever comforting my soul at length

to me, you are a superstar
a woman of many avatars
mom, I cannot thank you enough
for you have given me so much

SIBLING

fun and frolic all the time
we laughed, played, and teased
she was my partner in crime
when we were unleashed

feels like yesterday
what was long ago
I wish those days
come back once more

THOSE EYES

saw those eyes one day
they made my heart sway
like almond they were
me falling for her, oh dear

those big eyes dark brown
my knees keep bending on the
ground
they drew me in with such hypnosis
I felt like a man thirsty in an oasis

LOST MY HEART

my heart missed a beat
when I met you on that street
it is no longer mine
wish you to be my valentine
I lost my heart to you
there it will remain forever, it is so
true

SAY I DO

every now and then
offer her a rose
with emotions, passion and care
make her feel love is in the air
make her wish come true
keep saying I do I do

DAUGHTER

sent from heaven up above
a blessing for me to love
all bundled up, you were
looking like an angel, I swear

you touched my hand and did not let
go
that I still feel, what was long ago
time flies when we are together
we have so much fun with each
other

as you grow up, remember this
life is not always bliss
sometimes life may seem uphill
persist, it bends to your will
the road is full of obstacles, with
none to share
armed with courage, conquer it with
no fear

believe in your dreams, that is the
key
Princess I say, go make your own
destiny
my dear, I am always there with you
down here and from up above, it is
true

SMILE

your smile is so infectious
it comforts me in distress
in a life full of trials
all I need is that smile

TRUE FRIENDS

true friends
are hard to find
here are the virtues
keep them in mind

faithful and honest
those that stay in strife
are your friends
true friends for life

AN ANGEL

up there my angel awaits
sitting at the heaven gates
he waits for that day
when we two can play

a loyal friend he was
shaked hands with his paws
perfect companion for a stroll
he was truly a noble soul

THANKSGIVING

today is Thanksgiving Day
time for feasting on a Thursday
turkey and cranberry sauce on the
table
kids having fun, grownups telling
their fable

cornbread and pumpkin pie for
dessert
singing with friends, feels like a
concert
with family and friends
the day to give thanks
thank you for being there
in joy, struggles and despair

be grateful for all the good in your
life
look around, the world is full of strife
a prayer for His grace and might
with that, say your good night

BEST FRIEND

Zubair was my best friend
we played to our hearts content

he was like me
so well did we agree
always stood by my side
shielded me pushing them aside

I still miss him, wish him well
so many tales to share and tell
I hope we meet someday
and relive the glory days

SPIRITUALITY

THE ONE

different paths, destination is the same
so many prayers, what is in a name
mine is not better than his
He is, One and the same

SHIVA

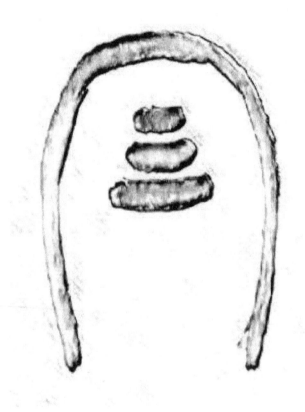

He is here, He is there
I believe He is everywhere
He is the beginning, He is the end
He is who we cannot comprehend

He is me; He is you
yet He is formless too
with Her by His side, a trident in hand
what a sight, so grand

He is handsome, she is beautiful
together they are all powerful
His abode is Kailash, He has names galore
Om Namah Shivay, let us chant once more

THE COSMIC DANCE

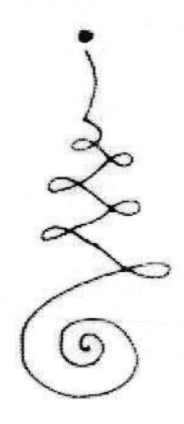

Shiva and Shakti

one is consciousness
other pure energy
together in synergy
they perform a cosmic dance
and in that trance
signs of creation.

MOUNT KAILASH

there is a mountain so mystical
a place so serene and magical
His abode, an immortal shrine
a place so ethereal and divine

blessed are those who go there
forever transformed, I swear
close your mind, meditate on this
you shall bear the fruit of bliss

KARMA

what is karma
your deeds paid back in full
remember to do good
then angels do your bid

what goes around comes around
remember, bad deeds bring you to
the ground
this is karma for you
good deeds, pay you out of the blue

SOUL

soul is like a mirror
look into it to see clearer
you may see things
sometimes scary, sometimes sad

good and bad is an ongoing strife
this is the fact of life
the eternal tussel is always there
conquer it by letting go off fear

ride your tempest of thoughts
show them you are the boss.

WHO IS HE

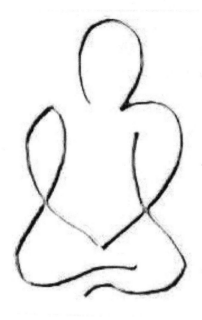

look for Him within
and all around you
He is in all His creation
from conception to annhilation.

STRINGS

what amazes me is this

we are pawns on a chess board
do not know who wins the game
we are puppets in a grand play
do not know the ending of the same

someone is making the moves
and pulling the strings
yet we think it is us
far from truth, we are all puzzled
beings

SHANKARACHARYA HILL

this was my daily drill
bow to the Shankaracharya hill
every morning as I stepped out
there it was without doubt

it would speak to me
I am with you, so said Thee
touching the blue sky
a temple dedicated to Thy

with folded hands I prayed
that memory has still stayed

THE PATRON SAINT OF KASHMIR

a mystic saint named Bhagwan
Gopinath
I was taught to follow his path

He spoke of three
mantras for you and me

be truthful
be honest
be candid

those who follow His principles
never falter and reach the pinnacle

THE SHRI CHAKRA AT HARI PARVAT

meditate on Her chakra someday
you will feel Her power, Her mystic
play
the energy is too much to take
this encounter will make you shake
it will give you the chills
and bow to Her you will

THE COSMOS

up there in space among the stars
a spine tingling experience it was
with black canvas and brushes in
hand
the creator painted a wonder so
grand

saw a sphere of blue, a tinge of
green
a spectacle I had never seen
in midst of shining stars
earth was a tiny blue dot
up there in space I was
drawn to splendor of the cosmos

NATURE

THE TULIP GARDEN OF KASHMIR

the beautiful tulip garden
on the foothills of Zabarwan
a marvel under the mountain
a sight to behold, a blessing of
heaven

beds of tulips
in a straight line
millions of cups, the dew adds to the
shine
a rainbow adding to the color
this experience is so divine

THE DAL LAKE

on the foothills of Shankaracharya
hill
a jewel in the crown, it is
the Dal Lake is scenic, so serene
sunrise is adding to the sheen

riding the shikaras is the norm
houseboats add to the charm
add floating gardens into the mix
a perfect spot for some clicks

the island of Char Chinar is unique
it has only four chinar trees
close by are the Mughal gardens
and the Hazratbal shrine
together they add to the divine

AUTUMN

leaves are turning
from green to brown
some are falling
on the ground
beautiful colors all around
green, red, orange, and brown

SEASON'S FIRST SNOW

I woke up to the falling of snow
silent yet spectacular in its glow
snowflakes are falling here and
there
greetings, season's first snow is here

they feel like stars falling down
little gems touching the ground
hot cocoa in hand
I go out to take a peek
some melt in my mouth
some kiss my cheek

a carpet of white by noon
I bow in awe to nature's boon
season's first snow is here
time for endless joy and prayer

SPRING

I long for the coming of spring
pleasure and fun that it brings
the melting of snow
the grass turning green

the chirping of birds
singing of robins at night
the hum of hummingbirds
and fog in the morning light

a sea of daffodils
on those hills
the dew on those tulips
just utter bliss

I long for the coming of spring
long for cherry blossoms to spring

THE BEACH

the sun is out
time to hit the beach
be one with the ocean
and ride the waves
in devotion

*those waves splashing back and
forth
welcoming you into the sea
a dolphin flying by in the north
there is no better place to be*

*build a castle on the sand
down by the blue sea
collect the shells in your hand
a good day's work if you ask me*

THE ROSE

of all the flowers out there
roses are best of them all
spreading fragrance in the air
in summer and early fall

they come in many colors
red, white yellow and many more
while red is for the lovers
orange lavender work well for décor

petals arranged in a symphony
swaying back and forth in a breeze
putting on a show so blissfully
God's creation at its best

THE DAFFODILS

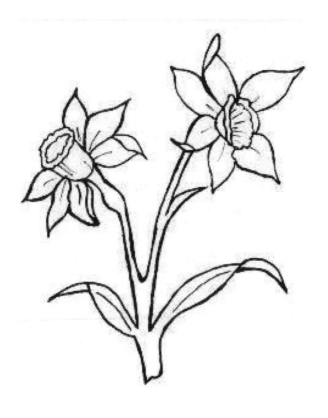

a sea of daffodils
yellow and white
up there on the hills
under the moonlight

swaying in the breeze they are
looking like a bunch of golden stars
sweet aroma is in the air
spreading breath of freshness
everywhere

THE SUNFLOWER

a bright yellow flower
radiant and gay
turns by the hour
follows the sun all day

a truly special flower
it stands high and tall
scentless is the sunflower
a source of joy for all

THE MARIGOLD

blooming sets of marigolds
an angelic sight to behold
yellow, orange, and brownish red
they look regal in a garden bed

fairies out there as well
on the marigold they dwell
all these butterflies in the air
seeking nectar here and there

INNER STRENGTH

THE ELITE

life offers you choices
need to hear those inner voices
want the best view in the woods
then scale the Everest, you should

this journey is all alone
do not fear the unknown
life may be too tough
hang in there, you must

the taste of victory is super sweet
congratulations, you are part of the
elite

THE EAGLE

ever seen an eagle in full flight
such grace and power, some sight
the king of birds flies alone
no one dare enter its zone

never shies away from a storm
an eagle never loses its calm
life lessons from an Eagle
be strong, graceful, and regal

the bird of Jove, always a trier
face your challenges to soar higher

THE ELEMENTS

passionate and dynamic, like fire
spread the light, is what I desire
deep and adaptable, like water
go with the flow, is what I offer

practical and grounded, like earth
stay firm, my two-penny's worth
lively and imperious, like air
full of vigor, such men are rare

fire water earth and air, my
constituents
always remember, be in your
elements

THE CODE

wear a smile on your face
a golden heart is your ace
roar like a lion
then this world will be mine
persevere like an ant
a mantra that one should chant
face your fears is the old adage
this is what is called courage

be true to who you are
then you will shine like a star
stay strong when pushed to the ground
then the world is your playground
life is to live and not to complain
die once not again and again
the naysayers will say nay
you just smile and say yay

A STEEP HILL

I set out to climb a steep hill
armed with nothing but my will
turned out tougher than I thought
in a pool of self-doubt I was caught

heard voices of quit all around
you cannot do it, back to the ground
all these thoughts in my head
still kept going, nevertheless

I finally reached my destination
a sigh of relief, a feeling of
completion
dream on, challenge yourself
surely you will find your inner self

THE LION

there is something about a lion
the awe, the strength, so divine
the mane that is golden brown
a majesty without a crown

the roar that is fierce and loud
one that stands out in a crowd
the walk that is full of pride
full of elegance, so dignified

bring out the lion in you
remember to take his que

THE HORSE

wild and a free spirit
qualities I love to inherit
I am a horsey
I am forever free

THE TRUE ME

the road ahead is rough
sometimes the going is tough
the cycle of life is such
do not ponder on it too much
patience is the key
show them your true me

WE WILL SURVIVE

in a time of suffering and despair
when the world seems beyond repair

human race struggling for survival
hope is the first step for revival

serve in this time of need
help, volunteer, and feed

light is just around the corner
human spirit is hard to conquer

muster your strength and resolve
in time, this too shall pass

BE STRONG

many out there may think
you will fumble, you will sink
that you may choke
that you are a joke

show them the real you
all the things that you can do
be strong, show them
they are so wrong

THE TREE

like a tree in the surround
be rooted to the ground
like a tree that stands strong and tall
do not fear challenges, proudly face
them all

sapling to tree, this journey is long
be patient, hastiness is simply
wrong
like a tree that provides shade
be that light for those that need aid

You have made it to the end.
A big thank you for being part of
this journey. May you follow your
beautiful heart and become the best
of what you can be.

About the Book

A Beautiful Heart
is a poetry collection
that takes you on a
journey of family bonds,
spirituality, nature and
inner strength.
A journey about you
expressed through
powerful feelings
and emotions.

About the Author

Born in Srinagar, Kashmir, Arun Warikoo lives in Princeton, New Jersey. He is a cyber security specialist by profession.

Arun Warikoo holds a Master's from University of Colorado, Boulder, a Diploma from CDAC, Bangalore, and a Bachelor's from Government College of Engineering, Aurangabad. He did his schooling from the Air Force Golden Jubilee Institute, New Delhi and Burn Hall School, Srinagar.

His poems are widely published in Poemist, and elsewhere. *A Beautiful Heart*, his first book, is a collection of forty five poems written on four themes: family bonds, spirituality, nature, and inner strength.

CPSIA information can be obtained
at www.ICGtesting.com
Printed in the USA
LVHW091542290121
677805LV00005B/283